About Demos

Demos is a greenhouse for new ideas which can improve the quality of our lives. As an independent think tank, we aim to create an open resource of knowledge and learning that operates beyond traditional party politics.

We connect researchers, thinkers and practitioners to an international network of **people changing politics**. Our ideas regularly influence government policy, but we also work with companies, NGOs, colleges and professional bodies.

Demos knowledge is organised around five themes, which combine to create new perspectives. The themes are democracy, learning, enterprise, quality of life and global change.

But we also understand that thinking by itself is not enough. Demos has helped to initiate a number of practical projects which are delivering real social benefit through the redesign of public services.

For Demos, the process is as important as the final product. We bring together people from a wide range of backgrounds to cross-fertilise ideas and experience. By working with Demos, our partners help us to develop sharper insight into the way ideas shape society.

www.demos.co.uk

For further information and subscription details please contact:

Demos
The Mezzanine
Elizabeth House
39 York Road
London SE1 7NQ

telephone: 020 7401 5330
email: mail@demos.co.uk
web: www.demos.co.uk

ISBN 1 84180 113 5
Typeset by Land & Unwin, Bugbrooke
Printed by Printflow, London
Series designed by Peter MacLeod

Open Source Democracy

How online communication is changing offline politics

Douglas Rushkoff

Foreword by Douglas Alexander, MP

Contents

Acknowledgements

Thanks to Tom Bentley and everyone at Demos for the opportunity to extend this enquiry to a new community of thinkers. Thanks also to my editorial assistant, Brooke Belisle, and to colleagues including Andrew Shapiro, Steven Johnson, Ted Byfield, Richard Barbrook, David Bennahum, Red Burns, Eugenie Furniss and Lance Strate.

Foreword

Douglas Alexander, MP

Man is still the most extraordinary computer of all.
– John F. Kennedy

The driving force of politics is, and has always been, the capacity it offers to change our lives, our communities and indeed our world. In the ebb and flow of contemporary political discourse it is sometimes easy to forget that what are at stake are the competing claims of political parties to our shared future. Yet the goal of any political party is not solely to secure power but to do so in order to secure a future which adheres to their conception of the good society. In defining our vision of that future the principles which inspired our forebears remain our touchstone – but the policies change to recognise the opportunities presented to each generation. To fail to identify these would make us solely a reactive rather than a proactive force, forever bound by events as they unfold rather than at the forefront of directing social change.

The phenomenon of interactive media is a case in point. A government which only seeks to grasp the technicalities of the evolving capacity of interactive media is one that will never be able truly to harness its capabilities. For progressive politics, recognising the parameters of possibility held out by interactive media is not solely about planning e-consultations or trying to ensure that every citizen has an email address. It presents a greater challenge – that of, to paraphrase the American writer Andrei Cherny, rethinking the rules of public life to fit the contours of the new Britain evolving before our eyes.

Thus in shaping our vision of the future we must not only be aware of the potential inherent in interactive media, but also recognise how the experience of these developments influences public life itself. It is in understanding this process that Douglas Rushkoff's pamphlet is a timely contribution. Here he argues that the way in which the internet encourages user activity can be a metaphor for reawakening a public appetite for civic engagement. Tracing the changes in the way in which the internet has been used, he highlights the way in which its impact can be felt beyond the computer screen.

Certainly at every election cycle in America we have seen the internet evolve in a bid to meet the new demands made of it. While in 2000 it provided an effective and innovative fundraising tool for Senator McCain, so in the run-up to the 2004 presidential elections we are now seeing how Howard Dean has used it to develop an organisational structure. The capacity of the Web to reach out to supporters across America and bring them together in regular meetings and campaign activities online has spilled over into their everyday lives with more than 300,000 and rising registered supporters meeting regularly in real time. In an age of falling turnout in elections across the globe, it is indeed powerful to see in action the capacity of the internet to bring people who live thousands of miles apart together in a virtual 'gathered community'. As Rushkoff argues, 'While it may not provide us with a template for sure-fire business and marketing solutions, the rise of interactive media does provide us with the beginnings of new metaphors for cooperation, new faith in the power of networked activity, and new evidence of our ability to participate actively in the authorship of our collective destiny.'

So what can we learn from this experience in our bid to create our version of the good society? Progressive politics is a politics which seeks to tackle inequality because we recognise that in extending opportunity to all the benefits accrue to all; that a fairer and more equal world is a better world because it is one in which all humanity flourishes. This is a politics grounded in the recognition that equality in society can only be driven by a process in which every person has their say – be they a millionaire, a maths teacher or a miner. Thus, creating a political environment in which all members of society participate on a wholly equal footing is not a question of electoral advantage but goes instead to the heart of social justice. Participation in the political process is thus a key guarantor of equality and opportunity – which is why in our current democratic context there is much to concern the left. Put simply, the falling turnout we face threatens not simply our electoral majority but our very capacity to create a truly egalitarian society. Without equal and open participation in decision-making processes, power and resource imbalances will always dictate outcomes making inequality perpetual.

There are those who seek to argue that reversing the falling turnout which characterises politics in the modern era is fighting a losing battle with an apathetic public. Yet as the American experience shows, there is clearly an enthusiasm for political expression. Similarly in the UK, from the Countryside Alliance to the Iraq marchers people have revealed themselves as intensely exercised about political issues. That this is not the story at the ballot box only makes the case for rethinking even more strongly the relationship between the state and the citizen.

Many of the old approaches and processes no longer work in a world increasingly stripped of deference. Rather than being concerned by this, we should welcome the growing confidence and interest in politics that this represents. In the contemporary era equality cannot be served by demanding a 'one-size-fits-all' or top-heavy approach to policy-making dominated by one group alone. Instead, the diversity of modern Britain requires a new way of thinking which acknowledges and empowers all citizens equally and so offers democratic structures which can facilitate a more responsive policy-making process. Thus our interest in government has been to create a democratic framework which shares out decision-making; to develop a pluralistic approach to politics which seeks diffusion of power to diverse groups ensuring that no one interest is served to the exclusion of another.

To that end we have devolved power through new institutions such as the Scottish Parliament and the Welsh Assembly so that together with the existing legislative bodies of the UK each can respond to the diversity of needs expressed by the people they serve. In this way each institution has started to develop the flexibility in decision-making that allows it to respond to its communities and thereby develop innovative ways of tackling issues, in essence becoming a 'laboratory' of policy-making. In the same way in which federalism in America allows each state to respond to the differing needs of the community they serve, so too here new ideas and new thinking have flourished.

Just like devolution, rather than being created and defined by any one user interactive media have evolved to meet a range of differing needs. The parameters of possibility of the internet are vast because it is the product not of a single point of reference but of its users seeking innovative ways to employ it for their own ends. In turn, it has brought together people across the world to work on solving common problems and bugs, creating a network of shared ideas and shared experiences from which we can all learn.

Thus the internet is both specific to the needs of its users and inherently a collectively engineered phenomenon. What makes this network succeed is a series of common protocols which facilitate but do not dictate the way in which the Web works. In the same way distributive democracy requires strong relationships between participants to ensure a feedback loop which allows innovation in policy-making to be diffused throughout every institution. Central government plays a key role in bringing together each of those institutions to ensure that devolution does not become an excuse for inequality because it brings together new thinking on common problems to ensure that everyone benefits.

As Andrei Cherny argues, the information age seeks political entities which are built on conversations, not monologues. Thus participation is no longer about listening to a hierarchical decision-making process but instead a cooperative experience for all citizens. In helping to advance the ideals of the egalitarian society, this form of 'offline' extension of the principles of 'online' action is to be welcomed. Yet, we must not lose sight that the driving force of this interactivity and its concomitant potential for extending egalitarian values is not the internet itself but the voice it gives to our civic disposition.

This is particularly relevant to the current interest in the role of the internet in the forthcoming presidential elections in America. As Mr Dean's internet campaign organiser, Zephyr Teachout, has stated, 'It gives people who would normally be lonely in the political process a way of finding each other.' In short, it is the ideas of Mr Dean which have generated the participation in his campaign rather than the internet itself. So we must be clear that this renewed interest in political activism is enabled, not engendered, by the internet.

At the heart of participation in all political activities – whether off- or online – will always be an appreciation of the difference that politics makes. It is important that in recognising the potential of the Web to help us re-engage the electorate we do not lose sight of the fact that voting is and will remain a political act. Technical innovations in how and when people interact with their elected representatives or cast their vote will only ever be one part of the answer. Our political challenge is in fact to affirm politics as a site of choices that matters to the lives of individuals, families and communities across the country – whether those choices are discussed on- or offline.

So too we must recognise that the 'gathered community' the internet offers is of use to political campaigning but not necessarily to democracy. Bringing together people who share a common identity or viewpoint is not the same as distributing democracy. The networks the Web creates allow us to bring people together who have shared interests – it starts from a point of shared agreement or reference. Democracy is about the resolution of competing claims – competing visions of the good society – in an arena which is open to all. Progressive politics thus requires structures which can engage people with differing views in a common dialogue where the legitimacy of participation is dependent on citizenship rather than access to a computer. At present the geographical basis on which this is organised generates an awareness of those competing choices because often they are literally on your doorstep. This forces politicians to deal with rival demands for resources in a way in which current political interactive media activity is only beginning to explore. Because of its very capacity to bring people together across space and time, using the Web to create democratic structures will inevitably change perceptions of the constituency of interest in question. In our enthusiasm over the potential of the internet to provide new ways of facilitating democratic engagement we must not lose our determination to recognise the challenges of accountability and accessibility for such e-frameworks as we do for our present offline democratic structures.

Clearly this is an exciting and important area of discussion for civic life and I welcome the work being done by Demos in this area. The internet has the potential to produce an information-rich world in which all citizens are able to communicate, educate and legislate in a way previously considered impossible. Similarly just as the Web continues to evolve and adjust to the changing needs of its users so our challenge now is to build on the foundations of the distributive democracy we have begun to fashion. These are not necessarily separate concerns, but our actions must be driven by our vision of the future rather than solely by a willingness to experiment. Thus as we seek to create a progressive agenda for this century, we must be resolute in our determination to harness these processes and their social and cultural impact to make real our version of the good society – a society which extends equality both on- and offline. As Daniel Bell notes, 'Technology, like art, is a soaring exercise of human imagination.'

Douglas Alexander is MP for Paisley South and the Cabinet Office minister whose responsibilities include e-government.

1. Introduction

The emergence of the interactive mediaspace may offer a new model for cooperation. Although it may have disappointed many in the technology industry, the rise of interactive media, the birth of a new medium, the battle to control it and the downfall of the first victorious camp, taught us a lot about the relationship of ideas to the media through which they are disseminated. Those who witnessed or, better, have participated in the development of the interactive mediaspace have a very new understanding of the way that cultural narratives are developed, monopolised and challenged. And this knowledge extends, by allegory and experience, to areas far beyond digital culture, to the broader challenges of our time.

As the world confronts the impact of globalism, newly revitalised threats of fundamentalism, and the emergence of seemingly irreconcilable value systems, generate a new reason to believe that living interdependently is not only possible, but preferable to the competitive individualism, ethnocentrism, nationalism and particularism that have characterised so much of late twentieth-century thinking and culture.

The values engendered by our fledgling networked culture may, in fact, help a world struggling with the impact of globalism, the lure of fundamentalism and the clash of conflicting value systems. Thanks to the actual and allegorical role of interactive technologies in our work and lives, we may now have the ability to understand many social and political constructs in very new contexts. We may now be able to launch the kinds of conversations that change the relationship of individuals, parties, creeds and nations to one another and to the world at large. These interactive communication technologies could even help us to understand autonomy as a collective phenomenon, a shared state that emerges spontaneously and quite naturally when people are allowed to participate actively in their mutual self-interest.

The emergence of the internet as a self-organising community, its subsequent co-option by business interests, the resulting collapse of the dot.com pyramid and the more recent self-conscious revival of interactive media's most participatory forums, serve as a case study in the politics of renaissance. The battle for control over new and little understood communication technologies has rendered transparent many of the agendas implicit in our political and cultural narratives. Meanwhile, the technologies themselves empower individuals to take part in the creation of new narratives. Thus, in an era when crass perversions of populism, and exaggerated calls for national security, threaten the very premises of representational democracy and free discourse, interactive technologies offer us a ray of hope for a renewed spirit of genuine civic engagement.

The very survival of democracy as a functional reality may be dependent upon our acceptance, as individuals, of adult roles in conceiving and stewarding the shape and direction of society. And we may get our best rehearsal for these roles online.

In short, the interactive mediaspace offers a new way of understanding civilisation itself, and a new set of good reasons for engaging with civic reality more fully in the face of what are often perceived (or taught) to be the many risks and compromises associated with cooperative behaviour. Sadly, thanks to the proliferation of traditional top-down media and propaganda, both marketers and politicians have succeeded in their efforts to turn neighbour against neighbour, city against city, and nation against nation. While such strategies sell more products, earn more votes and inspire a sense of exclusive salvation (we can't share, participate or, heaven forbid, collaborate with people whom we've been taught not to trust), they imperil what is left of civil society. They threaten the last small hope for averting millions of deaths in the next set of faith-justified oil wars.

As the mainstream mediaspace, particularly in the United States, becomes increasingly centralised and profit-driven, its ability to offer a multiplicity of perspectives on affairs of global importance is diminished. In America, broadcasting the Iraq war meant selling the Iraq war. Each of the media conglomerates broadcast the American regime's carefully concocted narrative, so much so that by the time the war actually began a Knight Ridder poll found that half of Americans believed that Iraqis had participated directly as hijackers on 11 September 2001. The further embedded among coalition troops that mainstream reporters were, the further embedded in the language and priorities of the Pentagon they became. Dispatches regularly referred to the deaths of Iraqi soldiers as the 'softening of enemy positions', bombing strikes as 'targets of opportunity', and civilian deaths as the now laughable 'collateral damage'. This was the propagandist motive for embedding reporters in the first place: when journalists' lives are dependent on the success of the troops with whom they are travelling, their coverage becomes skewed.

But this did not stop many of the journalists from creating their own weblogs, or blogs: internet diaries through which they could share their more candid responses to the bigger questions of the war. Journalists' personal entries provided a much broader range of opinions on both the strategies and motivations of all sides in the conflict than were available, particularly to Americans, on broadcast and cable television.

For an even wider assortment of perspectives, internet users were free to engage directly with the so-called enemy, as in the case of a blog called Dear Raed, written by what most internet experts came to regard as a real person living in Baghdad, voicing his opposition to the war. This daily journal of high aspirations for peace and a better life in Baghdad became one of the most read sources of information and opinion about the war on the web.

Clearly, the success of sites like Dear Raed stems from our increasingly complex society's need for a multiplicity of points of view on our most pressing issues, particularly when confronted by a mainstream mediaspace that appears to be converging on single, corporate and government-approved agenda. These alternative information sources are being given more attention and credence than they might actually deserve, but this is only because they are the only ready source of oppositional, or even independent thinking available. Those who choose to compose and disseminate alternative value systems may be working against the current and increasingly concretised mythologies of market, church and state, but they ultimately hold the keys to the rebirth of all three institutions in an entirely new context.

The communications revolution may not have brought with it either salvation for the world's stock exchanges or the technological infrastructure for a new global resource distribution system. Though one possible direction for the implementation of new media technology may be exhausted, its other myriad potentials beckon us once again. While it may not provide us with a template for sure-fire business and marketing solutions, the rise of interactive media does provide us with the beginnings of new metaphors for cooperation, new faith in the power of networked activity and new evidence of our ability to participate actively in the authorship of our collective destiny.

2. From Moses to modems: Demystifying the storytelling and taking control

We are living in a world of stories. We can't help but use narratives to understand the events that occur around us. The unpredictability of nature, emotions, social interactions and power relationships led human beings from prehistoric times to develop narratives that described the patterns underlying the movements of these forces. Although we like to believe that primitive people actually believed the myths they created about everything, from the weather to the afterlife, a growing camp of religious historians are concluding that early religions were understood much more metaphorically than we understand religion today. As Karen Armstrong explains in *A History of God*,[1] and countless other religious historians and philosophers from Maimonides to Freud have begged us to understand, the ancients didn't believe that the wind or rain were gods. They invented characters whose personalities reflected the properties of these elements. The characters and their stories served more as ways of remembering that it would be cold for four months before spring returned than as genuinely accepted explanations for nature's changes. The people were actively, and quite self-consciously, anthropomorphising the forces of nature.

As different people and groups competed for authority, narratives began to be used to gain advantage. Stories were no longer being used simply to predict the patterns of nature, but to describe and influence the courses of politics, economics and power. In such a world, stories compete solely on the basis of their ability to win believers; to be understood as real. When the Pharaoh or King was treated as if he were a god, his subjects were actively participating in the conceit. But he still needed to prove his potency in real ways, and at regular intervals, in order to ensure their continued participation. However, if the ruler could somehow get his followers to accept the story of his divine authority as historical fact, then he needed prove nothing. The story justified itself and was accepted as a reality.

In a sense, early civilisation was really just the process through which older, weaker people used stories to keep younger, stronger people from vying for their power. By the time the young were old enough to know what was going on, they were too invested in the system, or too physically weak themselves, to risk exposing the stories as myths. More positively, these stories provided enough societal continuity for some developments that spanned generations to take root.

The Old Testament, for example, is basically the repeated story of how younger sons attempt to outwit their fathers for an inherited birthright. Of course, this is simply an allegory for the Israelites' supplanting of the first-born civilisation, Egypt. But even those who understood the story as metaphor rather than historical fact continued to pass it on for the ethical tradition it contained: one of a people attempting to enact social justice rather than simply receive it.

Storytelling: communication and media

Since biblical times we have been living in a world where the stories we use to describe and predict our reality have been presented as truth and mistaken for fact. These narratives, and their tellers, compete for believers in two ways: through the content of the stories and through the medium or tools through which the stories are told. The content of a story might be considered the what, where the technology through which the story is transmitted can be considered the how. In moments when new technologies of storytelling develop, the competitive value of the medium can be more influential than the value of the message.

Exclusive access to the how of storytelling lets a storyteller monopolise the what. In ancient times, people were captivated by the epic storyteller as much for his ability to remember thousands of lines of text as for the actual content of the *Iliad* or *Odyssey*. Likewise, a television programme or commercial holds us in its spell as much through the magic of broadcasting technology as its script. Whoever has the power to get inside that magic box has the power to write the story we end up believing.

We don't call the stuff on television 'programming' for nothing. The people making television are not programming our TV sets or their evening schedules; they are programming us. We use the dial to select which programme we are going to receive and then we submit to it. This is not so dangerous in itself; but the less understanding and control we have over exactly what is fed to us through the tube, the more vulnerable we are to the whims of our programmers.

For most of us, what goes on in the television set is magic. Before the age of VCRs and camcorders it was even more so. The creation and broadcast of a television programme was a magic act. Whoever has his image in that box must be special. Back in the 1960s, Walter Cronkite used to end his newscast with the assertion: 'and that's the way it is.' It was his ability to appear in the magic box that gave him the tremendous authority necessary to lay claim to the absolute truth.

I have always recoiled when this rhetorical advantage is exploited by those who have the power to monopolise a medium. Consider, for example, a scene in the third Star Wars movie, *Return of the Jedi*. Luke and Hans Solo have landed on an alien moon and are taken prisoner by a tribe of little furry creatures called Ewoks. In an effort to win their liberation, Luke's two robots tell the Ewoks the story of their heroes' struggle against the dark forces of the Empire. C3PO, the golden android, relates the tale while little R2D2 projects holographic images of battling spaceships. The Ewoks are dazzled by R2's special effects and engrossed in C3PO's tale: the how and the what. They are so moved by the story that they not only release their prisoners but fight a violent war on their behalf! What if the Empire's villainous protector, Darth Vader, had arrived on the alien moon first and told his side of the story, complete with his own special effects?

Television programming communicates through stories and it influences us through its seemingly magical capabilities. The programmer creates a character we like and with whom we can identify. As a series of plot developments bring that character into some kind of danger, we follow him and within us a sense of tension arises.

This is what Aristotle called the rising arc of dramatic action. The storyteller brings the character, and his audience, into as much danger as we can tolerate before inventing a solution, the rescue, allowing us all to breathe a big sigh of relief. Back in Aristotle's day, this solution was called deus ex machina (God from the machine). One of the Greek gods would literally descend on a mechanism from the rafters and save the day. In an Arnold Schwarzenegger movie, the miraculous solution might take the form of a new, super-powered laser gun. In a commercial, the solution is, of course, the product being advertised.

TV commercials have honed this storytelling technique into the perfect 30-second package. A man is at work when his wife calls to tell him she's crashed the car. The boss comes in to tell him he just lost a big account, his bank statement shows he's in the red and his secretary quits. Now his head hurts. We've followed the poor guy all the way up Aristotle's arc of rising tension. We can feel the character's pain. What can he do? He opens the top desk drawer and finds his bottle of Brand A Pain Reliever and swallows the pills while an awe-inspiring hi-tech animation demonstrates the way the pill passes through his body. He, and we, are released from our torture.

In this passive and mysterious medium, when we are brought into a state of vicarious tension, we are more likely to swallow whichever pill and accept whatever solution the storyteller offers.

Interactivity: the birth of resistance

Interactive media changed this equation. Imagine if your father were watching that aspirin commercial back in 1955 on his old console television. Even if he suspected that he was watching a commercial designed to put him in a state of anxiety, in order to change the channel and remove himself from the externally imposed tension, he would have to move the popcorn off his lap, pull up the lever on his recliner, walk up to the television set and manually turn the dial. All that amounts to a somewhat rebellious action for a bleary-eyed television viewer. To sit through the rest of the commercial, however harrowing, might cost him only a tiny quantity of human energy until the pills come out of the drawer. The brain, being lazy, chooses the path of least resistance and Dad sits through the whole commercial.

Flash forward to 1990. A kid with a remote control in his hand makes the same mental calculation: an ounce of stress, or an infinitesimally small quantity of human effort to move his finger an eighth of an inch and he's free! The remote control gives viewers the power to remove themselves from the storyteller's spell with almost no effort. Watch a kid (or observe yourself) next time he channel surfs from programme to programme. He's not changing the channel because he's bored, but he surfs away when he senses that he's being put into an imposed state of tension.

The remote control breaks down the what. It allows a viewer to deconstruct the content of television media, and avoid falling under the programmer's spell. If a viewer does get back around the dial to watch the end of a programme, he no longer has the same captivated orientation. Kids with remotes aren't watching television, they are watching the television (the physical machine) playing 'television', putting it through its paces.

Just as the remote control allowed a generation to deconstruct the content of television, the video game joystick demystified its technology. Think back to the first time you ever saw a video game. It was probably Pong, that primitive black and white depiction of a ping-pong table, with a square on either side of the screen representing the bat and a tiny white dot representing the ball. Now, remember the exhilaration you felt at playing that game for the very first time. Was it because you had always wanted an effective simulation of ping-pong? Did you celebrate because you could practise without purchasing an entire table and installing it in the basement? Of course not. You were celebrating the simple ability to move the pixels on the screen for the first time. It was a moment of revolution! The screen was no longer the exclusive turf of the television broadcasters.

Thanks to the joystick, as well as the subsequent introduction of the VCR and camcorder, we were empowered to move the pixels ourselves. The TV was no longer magical. Its functioning had become transparent. Just as the remote control allowed viewers to deconstruct the content of storytelling, the joystick allowed the audience to demystify the technology through which these stories were being told.

Finally, the computer mouse and keyboard transformed a receive-only monitor into a portal. Packaged programming was no longer any more valuable, or valid, than the words we could type ourselves. The addition of a modem turned the computer into a broadcast facility. We were no longer dependent on the content of Rupert Murdoch or corporate TV stations, but could create and disseminate our own content. The internet revolution was a do-it-yourself revolution. We had deconstructed the content of media's stories, demystified its modes of transmission and learned to do it all for ourselves.

These three stages of development: deconstruction of content, demystification of technology and finally do-it-yourself or participatory authorship are the three steps through which a programmed populace returns to autonomous thinking, action and collective self-determination.

3. Electronic community: From birth to backlash

New forms of community were emerging that stressed the actual contributions of the participants, rather than whatever prepackaged content they had in common. In many cases, these contributions took the form not of ideas or text but technology itself.

The early interactive mediaspace was a gift economy (see Barbrook[2]). People developed and shared new technologies with no expectation of financial return. It was gratifying enough to see one's own email program or bulletin board software spread to thousands of other users. The technologies in use on the internet today, from browsers and POP email programs to streaming video, were all developed by this shareware community of software engineers. The University of Illinois at Urbana-Champaign, where Mosaic, the precursor to Netscape, was first developed was a hotbed of new software development. So were Cornell and MIT, as well as hundreds of more loosely organised hacker groups around the world.

Invariably, the software applications developed by this community stressed communication over mere data retrieval. They were egalitarian in design. IRC chats and USENET groups, for example, present every contributor's postings in the same universal ASCII text.

The internet was a text-only medium and its user was as likely to be typing into the keyboard as reading what was on screen. It is as if the internet's early developers released that this was not a medium for broadcasting by a few but for the expression of the many.

People became the content, a shift that had implications not just for the online community but for society as a whole. The notion of a group of people working together for a shared goal rather than financial self-interest was quite startling to Westerners whose lives had been organised around the single purpose of making money and achieving personal security. The internet was considered sexy simply because young people took an interest in it. People who developed internet applications in this way were called cyberpunks or hackers, and their antics were often equated with those of Wild West outlaws, hippies, Situationists and even communists.

But their organisation model was much more complex and potentially far-reaching than those of their countercultural predecessors. Many of these early technology and media pioneers would not have considered themselves to be part of a counterculture at all. Indeed, many new models for networked behaviour and collaborative engagement were developed at research facilities dedicated to the advancement of military technology. A US government policy requiring all firms working under Defense Department contracts to test their employees' blood and urine for illegal drug use led to a certain disconnection between most Silicon Valley firms and the majority of the fledgling computer counterculture. (In fact, of all the Silicon Valley firms, only Sun computing quite conspicuously refused to do drug testing on its employees.)

Whatever the applications envisioned for the communication technology being developed, the operating principles of the finished networking solutions, as well as the style of collaboration required to create them, offered up a new cultural narrative based in collective self-determination.

Online communities sprung up seemingly from nowhere. On the West Coast in the late 1980s one of Ken Kesey's Merry Pranksters,

Stewart Brand (now co-founder of the prestigious Global Business Network), conceived and implemented an online bulletin board called The Well (Whole Earth 'Lectronic Link). Within two years thousands of users had joined the dial-in computer conferencing system and were sharing their deepest hopes and fears with one another. Famous scientists, authors, philosophers and scores of journalists flocked to the site in order to develop their ideas collaboratively rather than alone. Meanwhile, as the internet continued to develop, online discussions in a distributed system called USENET began to proliferate. These were absolutely self-organising discussions about thousands of different topics. They themselves spawned communities of scientists, activists, doctors, and patients, among so many others, dedicated to tackling problems in collaboration across formerly prohibitive geographical and cultural divides.

The backlash

These new communities are perhaps the reason why the effects of the remote, joystick and mouse represented such a tremendous threat to business as usual. Studies in the mid-1990s showed that families with internet-capable computers were watching an average of nine hours less television per week. Even more frightening to those who depended on the mindless passivity of consumer culture, internet enthusiasts were sharing information, ideas and whole computer programs for free! Software known as 'freeware' and 'shareware' gave rise to a gift economy based on community and mutual self-interest. People were turning to alternative news and entertainment sources, which they didn't have to pay for. Worse, they were watching fewer commercials. Something had to be done. And it was.

It is difficult to determine exactly how intentional each of the mainstream media's attacks were on the development of the internet and the culture it spawned. Certainly, the many executives of media conglomerates who contacted my colleagues and me for advice throughout the 1990s were both threatened by the unchecked growth of interactive culture and anxious to cash in on these new developments. They were chagrined by the flow of viewers away from television programming, but they hoped this shift could be managed and ultimately exploited. While many existing content industries, such as the music recording industry, sought to put both individual companies and entire new categories out of business (such as Napster and other peer-to-peer networks), the great majority of executives did not want to see the internet entirely shut down. It was, in fact, the US government, concerned about the spread of pornography to minors and encryption technology to rogue nations, that took more direct actions against the early internet's new model of open collaboration.

Although many of the leaders and top shareholders of global media conglomerates felt quite threatened by the rise of new media, their conscious efforts to quell the unchecked spread of interactive technology were not the primary obstacles to the internet's natural development. A review of articles quoting the chiefs at TimeWarner, Newscorp and Bertelsman reveals an industry either underestimating or simply misunderstanding the true promise of interactive media.

The real attacks on the emerging new media culture were not orchestrated by old men from high up in glass office towers but arose almost as systemic responses from an old media culture responding to the birth of its successor. It was both through the specific, if misguided, actions of some media executives, as well as the much more unilateral response of an entire media culture responding to a threat to the status quo, that mainstream media began to reverse the effects of the remote, the joystick and the mouse.

Borrowing a term from 1970s' social science, media business advocates declared that we were now living in an 'attention economy'. True enough, the mediaspace might be infinite but there are only so many hours in a day during which potential audience members might be viewing a programme. These units of human time became known as eyeball-hours, and pains were taken to create TV shows and web sites 'sticky' enough to engage those eyeballs long enough to show them an advertisement.

Perhaps coincidentally, the growth of the attention economy was accompanied by an increase of concern over the attention spans of young people. Channel surfing and similar behaviour became equated with a very real but variously diagnosed childhood illness called Attention Deficit Disorder. Children who refused to pay attention were (much too quickly) drugged with addictive amphetamines before the real reasons for their adaptation to the onslaught of commercial messages were even considered.

The demystification of media, enabled by the joystick and other early interactive technologies, was quickly reversed through the development of increasingly opaque computer interfaces. While early DOS computer users tended to understand a lot about how their computers stored information and launched programs, later operating systems such as Windows 95 put more barriers in place. Although these operating systems make computers easier to use in some ways, they prevent users from gaining access or command over its more intricate processes. Now, to install a new program, users must consult the 'wizard'. What better metaphor do we need for the remystification of the computer? Computer literacy no longer means being able to programme a computer, but merely knowing how to use software such as Microsoft Office.

Finally, the do-it-yourself ethic of the internet community was replaced by the new value of commerce. The communications age was rebranded as the information age, even though the internet had never really been about downloading files or data, but about communicating with other people. The difference was that information, or content, unlike real human interaction, could be bought and sold. It was a commodity. People would pay, it was thought, for horoscopes, stock prices and magazine articles. When selling information online didn't work, businesspeople instead turned to selling real products online. Horoscope.com and online literary journals gave way to Pets.com and online bookstores. The e-commerce boom was ignited. Soon the internet became the World Wide Web. Its opaque and image-heavy interfaces made it increasingly one-way and read-only, more conducive to commerce than communication. The internet was reduced to a direct marketing platform.

The burst of the bubble and the re-emergence of community

Few e-commerce companies made any money selling goods, but the idea that they could was all that mattered. When actual e-commerce didn't work, the internet was rebranded yet again as an investment platform. The Web was to be the new portal through which the middle class could invest in the stock market. And which stocks were they to invest in? Internet stocks, of course! Like any good pyramid scheme, everyone was in on it. Or at least they thought they were.

News stories about online communities such as The Well, or even discussion groups for breast cancer survivors were soon overshadowed by those about daring young entrepreneurs launching multi-million-dollar IPOs (Initial Price Offerings of formerly private stock on public exchanges such as the NYSE or NASDAQ.) Internet journalism, written by option-holding employees of media conglomerates, moved from the culture section to the business pages and the dot.com pyramid scheme became the dominant new media story.

A medium born out of the ability to break through packaged stories was now being used to promote a new, equally dangerous one: the great pyramid. A smart kid writes a business plan. He finds a few 'angel' investors to back him up long enough to land some first-level investors. Below them on the pyramid are several more rounds of investors, until the investment bank gets involved. Another few levels of investors buy in until the decision is made to go public. Of course, by this point, the angels and other early investors are executing their exit strategy. It used be known as a carpet bag. In any case they're gone and the investing public is left holding the soon-to-be-worthless shares.

Tragically, but perhaps luckily, the dot.com bubble burst along with the story being used to keep it inflated. The entire cycle, the birth of a new medium, the battle to control it and the downfall of the first victorious camp, taught us a lot about the relationship of stories to the technologies through which they are disseminated. And the whole ordeal may have given us an opportunity for renaissance.

Back here in the real world, the internet is doing just fine. Better than ever. The World Wide Web, whose rather opaque platform ascended primarily for its ability to serve as an online catalogue, has been adapted to serve many of the internet's original, more technologically primitive functions. USENET discussions have been reborn as web-based bulletin boards such as Slashdot, and Metafilter. Personal daily diaries known as weblogs have multiplied by the thousands. Blogger.com provides a set of publishing tools that allows even a novice to create a weblog, automatically add content to a web site or organise links, commentary and open discussions. In the short time Blogger has been available, it has fostered an interconnected community of tens of thousands of users. These people don't simply surf the Web. They are now empowered to create it.

Rising from the graveyard of failed business plans, these collaborative communities of authors and creators are the true harbingers of cultural and perhaps political renaissance.

4. The opportunity for renaissance

The birth of the internet was interpreted by many as a revolution. Those of us in the counterculture saw in the internet an opportunity to topple the storytellers who had dominated our politics, economics, society and religion – in short our very reality – and to replace their stories with those of our own. It was a beautiful and exciting sentiment, but one as based in a particular narrative as any other. Revolutions simply replace one story with another. The capitalist narrative is replaced by that of the communist; the religious fundamentalist's replaced by the agnostic's. The means may be different, but the rewards are the same. So is the exclusivity of their distribution. That's why they're called revolutions – we're just going in a circle.

This is why it might be more useful to understand the proliferation of interactive media as an opportunity for renaissance: a moment when we have the ability to step out of the story altogether. Renaissances are historical instances of widespread recon-textualisation. People in a variety of different arts, philosophies and sciences have the ability to reframe their reality. Renaissance literally means 'rebirth'. It is the rebirth of old ideas in a new context. A renaissance is a dimensional leap, when our perspective shifts so dramatically that our understanding of the oldest, most fundamental elements of existence changes. The stories we have been using no longer work.

Take a look back at what we think of as the original Renaissance, the one we were taught in school. What were the main leaps in perspective? One example is the use of perspective in painting. Artists developed the technique of the vanishing point and with it the ability to paint three-dimensional representations on two-dimensional surfaces. The character of this innovation is subtle but distinct. It is not a technique for working in three dimensions; it is not that artists moved from working on canvas to working with clay. Rather, perspective painting allows an artist to relate between dimensions: representing three-dimensional objects on a two-dimensional plane.

Another example is calculus, another key Renaissance invention. Calculus is a mathematical system that allows us to derive one dimension from another. It is a way of describing curves with the language of lines, and spheres with the language of curves. The leap from arithmetic to calculus was not just a leap in our ability to work with higher dimensional objects, but a leap in our ability to relate the objects of one dimension to the objects of another. It was a shift in perspective that allowed us to orient ourselves to mathematical objects from beyond the context of their own dimensionality.

The other main features of the Renaissance permitted similar shifts in perspective. Circumnavigation of the globe changed our relationship between the planet we live on and the maps we used to describe it. The maps still worked, they just described a globe instead of a plane. Anyone hoping to navigate a course had to be able to relate a two-dimensional map to the new reality of a three-dimensional planet.

Similarly, the invention of moveable type and the printing press changed the relationship of author and audience to text. The creation of a manuscript was no longer a one-pointed affair. The creation of the first manuscript still was, but now it could be replicated and distributed to everyone. It was still one story, but now was subject to a multiplicity of individual perspectives. This innovation alone changed the landscape of religion in the Western world. Individual interpretation of the Bible led to the collapse of church authority and the unilateral nature of its decrees. Everyone demanded his or her own relationship to the story.

Our electronic renaissance

In all these cases, people experienced a very particular shift in their relationship to, and understanding of, dimensions. Understood this way, a renaissance is a moment of reframing. We step out of the frame as it is currently defined and see the whole picture in a new context. We can then play by new rules.

It is akin to the experience of a computer game player. At first, a gamer will play a video or computer game by the rules. He'll read the manual, if necessary, then move through the various levels of the game. Mastery of the game, at this stage, means getting to the end: making it to the last level, surviving, becoming the most powerful character or, in the case of a simulation game, designing and maintaining a thriving family, city or civilisation. For many gamers, this is as far as it goes.

Some gamers, though – usually after they've mastered this level of play – will venture out onto the internet in search of other fans or user groups. There, they will gather the cheat codes that can be used to acquire special abilities within the game, such as invisibility or an infinite supply of ammunition. When the gamer returns to the game with his secret codes, is he still playing the game or is he cheating? From a renaissance perspective he is still playing the game, albeit a different one. His playing field has grown from the CD on which the game was shipped to the entire universe of computers where these secret codes and abilities can be discussed and shared. He is no longer playing the game, but a meta-game. The inner game world is still fun, but it is distanced by the gamer's new perspective, much in the way we are distanced from the play-within-a-play in one of Shakespeare's comedies or dramas. And the meta-theatrical convention gives us new perspective on the greater story as well. Gaming, as a metaphor but also as a lived experience, invites a renaissance perspective on the world in which we live. Perhaps gamers and their game culture have been as responsible as anyone for the rise in expressly self-similar forms of television like Beavis and Butt-head, The Simpsons and Southpark. The joy of such programmes is not the relief of reaching the climax of the linear narrative, but rather the momentary thrill of making connections. The satisfaction is in recognising which bits of media are being satirised at any given moment. It is an entirely new perspective on television, where programmes exist more in the form of Talmudic commentary: perspectives on perspectives on perspectives. We watch screens within screens, constantly reminded, almost as in a Brecht play, of the artifice of storytelling. It is as if we are looking at a series of proscenium arches, and are being invited as an audience to consider whether we are within a proscenium arch ourselves.

The great Renaissance was a simple leap in perspective. Instead of seeing everything in one dimension, we came to realise there was more than one dimension on which things were occurring. Even the Elizabethan world picture, with its concentric rings of authority – God, king, man, animals – reflects this newfound way of contending with the simultaneity of action of many dimensions at once. A gamer stepping out onto the internet to find a cheat code certainly reaches this first renaissance's level of awareness and skill.

But what of the gamer who then learns to programme new games for himself? He, we might argue, has stepped out of yet another frame into our current renaissance. He has deconstructed the content of the game, demystified the technology of its interface and now feels ready to open the codes and turn the game into a do-it-yourself activity. He has moved from a position of a receiving player to that of a deconstructing user. He has assumed the position of author, himself. This leap to authorship is precisely the character and quality of the dimensional leap associated with today's renaissance.

The evidence of today's renaissance is at least as profound as that of the one that went before. The sixteenth century saw the successful circumnavigation of the globe via the seas. The twentieth century saw the successful circumnavigation of the globe from space. The first pictures of earth from space changed our perspective on this sphere for ever. In the same century, our dominance over the planet was confirmed not just through our ability to travel around it, but to destroy it. The atomic bomb (itself the result of a rude dimensional interchange between submolecular particles) gave us the ability to author the globe's very destiny. Now, instead of merely being able to comprehend 'God's creation', we could actively control it. This is a new perspective.

We also have our equivalent of perspective painting, in the invention of the holograph. The holograph allows us to represent not just three, but four dimensions on a two-dimensional plate. When the viewer walks past a holograph she can observe the three-dimensional object over a course of time. A bird can flap its wings in a single picture. But, more importantly for our renaissance's purposes, the holographic plate itself embodies a new renaissance principle. When the plate is smashed into hundreds of pieces, we do not find that one piece contains the bird's wing, and another piece the bird's beak. Each piece of the plate contains a faint image of the entire subject. When the pieces are put together, the image achieves greater resolution. But each piece contains a representation of the totality. This leap in dimensional understanding is now informing disciplines as diverse as brain anatomy and computer programming.

Our analogy to calculus is the development of systems theory, chaos maths and the much celebrated fractal. Confronting non-linear equations on their own terms for the first time, mathematicians armed with computers are coming to new understandings of the way numbers can be used to represent the complex relationships between dimensions. Accepting that the surfaces in our world, from coastlines to clouds, exhibit the properties of both two- and three-dimensional objects (just what is the surface area of a cloud?) they came up with ways of working with and representing objects with fractional dimensionality.

Using fractals and their equations, we can now represent and work with objects from the natural world that defy Cartesian analysis. We also become able to develop mathematical models that reflect many more properties of nature's own systems, such as self-similarity and remote high leverage points. Again, we find that this renaissance is characterised by the ability of an individual to reflect, or even affect, the grand narrative. To write the game.

Finally, our renaissance's answer to the printing press is the computer and its ability to network. Just as the printing press gave everyone access to readership, the computer and internet give everyone access to authorship. The first Renaissance took us from the position of passive recipient to active interpreter. Our current renaissance brings us from the role of interpreter to the role of author. We are the creators.

As game programmers instead of game players, the creators of testimony rather than the believers in testament, we begin to become aware of just how much of our reality is open source and up for discussion. So much of what seemed like impenetrable hardware is actually software and ripe for reprogramming. The stories we use to understand the world seem less like explanations and more like collaborations. They are rule sets, only as good as their ability to explain the patterns of history or predict those of the future.

Consider the experience of a cartographer attempting to hold a conversation with a surfer. They both can claim intimate knowledge of the ocean, but from vastly different perspectives. While the mapmaker understands the sea as a series of longitude and latitude lines, the surfer sees only a motion of waves that are not even depicted on the cartographer's map. If the cartographer were to call out from the beach to the surfer and ask him whether he is above or below the 43rd parallel, the surfer would be unable to respond. The mapmaker would have no choice but to conclude that the surfer was hopelessly lost. But if any of us were asked to choose who we would rather rely on to get us back to shore, most of us would pick the surfer. He experiences the water as a system of moving waves and stands a much better chance of navigating a safe course through them. Each surfer at each location and each moment of the day experiences an entirely different ocean. The cartographer experiences the same map no matter what. He has a more permanent model, but his liability is his propensity to mistake his map for the actual territory.

The difference between the cartographer's and the surfer's experience of the ocean is akin to pre- and post-renaissance relationships to story. The first relies on the most linear and static interpretations of the story in order to create a static and authoritative template through which to glean its meaning. The latter relies on the living, moment-to-moment perceptions of its many active interpreters to develop a way of relating to its many changing patterns. Ultimately, in a cognitive process not unlike that employed by a chaos mathematician, the surfer learns to recognise the order underlying what at first appears to be random turbulence. Events, images and arrangements that might otherwise have appeared to be unrelated are now, thanks to a world view that acknowledges discontinuity, revealed to be connected. To those unfamiliar with this style of pattern recognition, the connections they draw may appear to be as unrelated as a fortune-teller's tea leaves or Tarot cards are from the future events she predicts. Nonetheless, the surfer understands each moment and event in his world as a possible reflection on any other aspect or moment in the entire system.

What gets reborn

The renaissance experience of moving beyond the frame allows everything old to look new again. We are liberated from the maps we have been using to navigate our world and free to create new ones based on our own observations. This invariably leads to a whole new era of competition. Renaissance may be a rebirth of old ideas in a new context, but which ideas get to be reborn?

The first to recognise the new renaissance will compete to have their ideologies be the ones that are rebirthed in this new context. This is why, with the emergence of the internet, we saw the attempted rebirth (and occasional stillbirth) of everything from paganism to libertarianism, and communism to psychedelia. Predictably, the financial markets and consumer capitalism, the dominant narratives of our era, were the first to commandeer successfully the renaissance. But they squandered their story on a pyramid scheme (indeed, the accelerating force of computers and networks tends to force any story to its logical conclusion) and now the interactive renaissance is once again up for grabs.

Perhaps the most valuable idea to plant now, into the post-renaissance society of tomorrow, is the very notion of renaissance itself. Interactivity, both as an allegory for a healthier relationship to cultural programming, and as an actual implementation of a widely accessible authoring technology, reduces our dependence on fixed narratives while giving us the tools and courage to develop narratives together. The birth of interactive technology has allowed for a sudden change of state. We have witnessed together the wizard behind the curtain. We can all see, for this moment anyway, how so very much of what we have perceived of as reality is, in fact, merely social construction. More importantly, we have gained the ability to enact such wizardry ourselves.

The most ready examples of such suddenly received knowledge come to us from the mystics. Indeed, many early cyber-pioneers expressed their insights (see my *Cyberia* for examples[3]) in mystical language coining terms such as 'technoshamanism' and 'cyberdelia'. Indeed, in some ways it does feel as though our society were at the boundaries of a mystical experience, when we have a glimpse of the profoundly arbitrary nature of the stories we use to organise and explain the human experience. It is at precisely these moments that the voyager wonders: 'what can I tell myself – what I can write down that will make me remember this experience beyond words?'

Of course, most of these mystical scribblings end up being over-simplified platitudes such as 'all is one' or 'I am God'. Those that rise above such clichés, such as the more mystical tractates of Ezekiel or Julian of Norwich, defy rational analysis or any effort at comprehension. Our only choice, in such a situation, might be to attempt to preserve just the initial insight that our maps are mere models, and that we have the ability to draw new ones whenever we wish.

This is why the scientists, mathematicians, engineers, business-people, religious and social organisers of the late twentieth century, who have adopted a renaissance perspective on their fields, have also proclaimed their insights to be so categorically set apart from the work of their predecessors. Chaos mathematicians (and the economists who depend on them) regard systems theory as an entirely new understanding of the inner workings of our reality. They are then celebrated on the pages of the *New York Times* for declaring that our universe is actually made up of a few simple equations called cellular-automata. Scientists find themselves abandoning a theory of anthill organisation that depends on commands from the queen, and replacing it with a bottom-up model of emergent organisation that depends on the free flow of information between every member of the colony.

More importantly, however, these flashes of insight and radical reappraisal of formerly sacrosanct ideas are followed not by a retrenchment but by a new openness to reflection, collaboration and change. The greatest benefit of a shift in operating model appears to be the recollection that we are working with a mere model.

11 September 2001: coping by retreat into a world view

More than any particular map or narrative we might develop, we need to retain the crucial awareness that any and all of these narratives are mere models for behavioural, social, economic or political success. Though provisionally functional, none of them are absolutely true. To mistake any of them for reality would be to mistake the map for the territory. This, more than anything, is the terrible lesson of the twentieth century. Many people, institutions and nations have yet to adopt strategies that take this lesson into account.

The oil industry and its representatives (some now elected in government) are, for example, incapable of understanding a profit model that does not involve the exploitation of fixed and limited resources. They continue to push the rest of the industrialised world towards the unnecessary bolstering of cooperative, if oppressive dictatorships, as well as the wars these policies invariably produce. The chemical and agriculture industries, incapable of envisioning a particular crop as anything but a drug-addicted, genetically altered species, cannot conceive of the impact of their innovations on the planet's topsoil or ecosystems. In more readily appreciated examples, the Church of England is still consumed with its defence of the literal interpretation of biblical events, and many fundamentalists sects in the United States still fight, quite successfully, to prevent the theory of evolution from being taught in state schools.

Although the terrorist attacks on the United States can find their roots, at least partially, in a legacy of misguided American foreign and energy policy decisions, they have also increased our awareness of a great chasm between peoples with seemingly irreconcilable stories about the world and humankind's role within it. And the lines between these world views are anything but clear.

Hours after the attacks, two of America's own fundamentalist ministers, Jerry Falwell and Pat Robertson, were quick to fit the tragic events into their own concrete narrative for God's relationship to humankind. Unable, or unwilling, to understand the apocalyptic moment as anything but the wrath of God, they blamed the feminists, homosexuals and civil libertarians of New York City for having brought this terrible but heavenly decree on themselves.

In a less strident but equally fundamentalist impulse, many American patriots interpreted the attacks as the beginning of a war against our nation's sacred values. This was to be seen as a war against capitalism and a free society. As American flags were raised in defiance of our Middle Eastern antagonists, just as many American freedoms were sacrificed to the new war on terrorism. Our nationalism overshadowed our national values, but our collective story was saved from deconstruction.

Meanwhile, free-market capitalism's stalwarts, who had already suffered the collapse of the dot.com bubble and the faith-challenging reality of an economic recession, were also reeling from the attack on their most visible symbol of global trade. With its dependence on perpetual expansion, the story of global capitalism was not helped by this sure sign of resistance. Might the world not really be ready to embrace the World Trade Organisation's gifts? With a utopian future of global economic prosperity as central to its basic premise as any fundamentalist vision of a perfect past era in harmony with God, believers in the capitalist narrative responded the only way they could. They sought a war to defend their story.

The most injurious rupture, of course, was to the narrative we use to feel safe and protected in an increasingly global society. The attacks on the Pentagon and World Trade Center, pinpointed, devastating, and worst of all perfectly executed, challenged the notion that we were the world's singularly invincible nation. The people we appointed to protect us had proved their inability to do so. President Bush's quick rise to an over 90 per cent popularity rating shows just how much we needed to believe in his ability to provide us with the omnipotent fatherly protection that his rhetoric commanded. But like a child realising that his parents can't save him from the bully at school, Americans were forced to consider that our leaders, our weapons and our wealth offer only so much insulation from a big bad world.

Our nurtured complacency and our sense of absolute security had always been unfounded, of course. But waking up to the great existential dilemma as suddenly as we did was a traumatic experience. It led us to revert to old habits. Anti-Semites (and latent anti-Semites) around the world used the catastrophe as new evidence of the 'Jewish problem'. Tsarist and Nazi propaganda books, such as *Protocols of the Elders of Zion*, hit the bestseller lists in countries like Saudi Arabia where they are still being published by official government presses. Newspaper stories revived blood libel (that Jews drink the blood of murdered non-Jewish teens) and spread the disinformation that Jews were warned about the attacks by their rabbis through special radios they keep in their homes. Indeed, such informational treachery is nothing new. But in the destabilised atmosphere of disrupted narrative, it spread faster, wider and with greater effect than it otherwise would have.

Efforts to package America's New War on news channels like CNN further alienated the more cynical viewers from the mainstream account of what had happened. Conspiracy theorists, Web activists and open-minded leftists, already suspicious of the narratives presented through television, found themselves falling prey to a falsified email letter from a Brazilian schoolteacher claiming that video footage of Palestinians celebrating the attacks had actually been shot years earlier during the Gulf War. Like any other narrative, the extreme counterculture's saga of a 'new world order', directed by the Bush family, had to be wrapped around the new data.

Meanwhile, many Jews and Christians who hadn't even thought about their religion or their ethnicity for years found themselves instinctively asking: 'how will this impact Israel?' or 'is the Armageddon upon us?' They bought memberships in religious institutions for the first time in decades, and packed into their churches and synagogues looking for reassurance, for a way to fit these catastrophes into a bigger story. Like everyone else, they hoped to reconstruct the narrative that had been shattered.

But surely our world views, political outlooks and religions aren't functioning at their best when they provide pat answers to life's biggest questions. The challenge to all thinking people is to resist the temptation to fall into yet another polarised, nationalist or, God forbid, holy posture. Rather than retreating into the simplistic and childlike, if temporarily reassuring, belief that the answers have already been written along with the entire human story, we must resolve ourselves to participate actively in writing the story ourselves. It is not enough to go back to our old models, particularly when they have been revealed to be inadequate at explaining the complexity of the human condition. It is too late for the Western world to retreat into Christian fundamentalism, accelerating global conflict in an effort to bring on the messianic age. It is too late to push blindly towards a purely capitalist model of human culture. There is simply too much evidence that the short-term bottom line does not serve the needs of people or the environment. There are too many alternative values and cultural threads surrendered to profit efficiency that may yet prove vital to our cultural ecosystem.

Instead, we must forge ahead into the challenging but necessary task of inventing new models ourselves, using the collaborative techniques learned over the past decade, and based in the real evidence around us.

5. Networked democracy

The values engendered by our fledgling networked culture may, in fact, prove quite applicable to the broader challenges of our time and help a world struggling with the impact of globalism, the lure of fundamentalism and the clash of conflicting value systems. The very survival of democracy as a functional reality is dependent upon our acceptance, as individuals, of adult roles in conceiving and stewarding the shape and direction of society.

Religions and ideologies are terrific things, so long as no one actually believes in them. While absolute truths may exist, it is presumptuous for anyone to conclude he has found and comprehended one. True, the adoption of an absolutist frame of reference serves many useful purposes. An accepted story can unify an otherwise diverse population, provide widespread support for a single regime and reassure people in times of stress. Except for the resulting ethnocentrism, repression of autonomy and stifling of new ideas, such static templates can function well for quite a while. Dictators from Adolf Hitler to Idi Amin owed a good part of their success to their ability to develop ethnically based mythologies that united their people under a single sense of identity. The biblical myth of Jacob and his sons served to unify formerly non-allied desert tribes (with the same names as Jacob's sons) in ancient Sinai. They not only conquered much of the region, but created a fairly stable regime for centuries.

So these stories enable a certain kind of functionality. Their relative stasis, if protected against the effects of time by fundamentalists, can allow for the adoption and implementation of long-term projects that span generations, even centuries. But when one group's absolute truth bumps up against another group's absolute truth, only conflict can result.

New technologies, global media, and the spread of international corporate conglomerates have forced just such a clash of world views. While cultures have been reckoning with the impact of cosmopolitanism since even before the first ships crossed the Mediterranean, today's proliferation of media, products and their associated sensibilities, as well as their migration across formerly discreet boundaries, are unprecedented in magnitude.

Globalism, at least as it is envisioned by the more expansionist advocates of free market capitalism, only exacerbates the most dangerously retrograde strains of xenophobia. The market's global aspirations (as expressed by Global Business Network co-founder Peter Schwartz's slogan 'Open markets good. Closed markets bad. Tattoo it on your forehead'[4]) amount to a whitewash of regional cultural values. They are as reductionist as the tenets of any fundamentalist religion. In spite of the strident individualism of this brand of globalist rhetoric, it leaves no room for independent thinking or personal choice, except insofar as they are permitted by one's consumption decisions or the way one chooses to participate in the profit-making game. Mistaking the arbitrary and man-made rules of the marketplace for a precondition of the natural universe, corporate capitalism's globalist advocates believe they are liberating the masses from the artificially imposed restrictions of their own forms of religion and government. Perceiving the free market model as the way things really are, they ignore their own fabrications, while seeing everyone else's models as impediments to the natural and rightful force of evolution.

As a result, globalism, to almost anyone but a free market advocate, has come to mean the spread of the Western corporate value system to every other place in the world. Further, the bursting of the dot.com bubble, followed by the revelation of corporate malfeasance and insider trading, exposed corporate capitalism's dependence on myths; stories used to captivate and distract the public while the storytellers ran off with the funds. The spokespeople for globalism began to be perceived as if they were the fifteenth-century Catholic missionaries that preceded the Conquistadors, preparing indigenous populations for eventual colonisation. The free market came to be understood as just another kind of marketing. Globalism was reduced, in the minds of most laypeople, to one more opaque mythology used to exploit the uninitiated majority.

Networked democracy: learning from natural interconnectivity

The current renaissance offers new understandings of what it might mean to forge a global society that transcends the possibilities described by the language of financial markets. It might not be too late to promote a globalism modelled on cooperation instead of competition, and on organic interchange instead of financial transaction.

Again, our renaissance insights and inventions aid us in our quest for a more dimensionalised perspective on our relationship to one another. Rather famously the first Renaissance elevated the Catholic mass into a congregation of Protestant readers. Thanks to the printing press and the literacy movement that followed, each person could enjoy his or her own personal relationship to texts and the mythologies they described. Our own renaissance offers us the opportunity to enhance the dimensionality of these relationships even further, as we transform from readers into writers.

It's no coincidence that early internet users became obsessed with the fractal images they were capable of producing. The reassuring self-similarity of these seemingly random graphs of non-linear equations evoked the shapes of nature. One simple set of fractal equations, iterated through a computer, could produce a three-dimensional image of a fern, a coastline or a cloud. Zooming in on one small section revealed details and textures reflective of those on other levels of magnification. Indeed, each tiny part appeared to reflect the whole.

For early internet users, sitting alone in their homes or offices, connected to one another only by twisted pairs of copper phone lines, the notion of being connected, somehow, in the manner of a fractal was quite inspiring. They began to study new models of interconnectivity and group mind, such as James Lovelock's Gaia hypothesis and Rupert Sheldrake's theory of morphogenesis, to explain and confirm their growing sense of non-local community. By the mid-1990s many internet users began to see the entire planet as a single organism, with human beings as the neurons in a global brain. The internet, according to this scheme, was the neural network being used to wire up this brain so that it could function in a coordinated fashion. In another model for group mind, this time celebrated among the rave counterculture, this connectivity was itself a pre-existing state. The internet was merely a metaphor, or outward manifestation, of a psychic connection between human beings that was only then being realised: the holographic reality.

As functioning models for cooperative activity, these notions are not totally unsupported by nature. Biologists studying complex systems have observed coordinated behaviours between creatures that have no hierarchical communication scheme, or even any apparent communication scheme whatsoever. The coral reef, for example, exhibits remarkable levels of coordination even though it is made up of millions of tiny individual creatures. Surprisingly, perhaps, the strikingly harmonious behaviour of the collective does not repress the behaviour of the individual. In fact the vast series of interconnections between the creatures allows any single one of them to serve as a 'remote high leverage point' influencing the whole. When one tiny organism decides it is time for the reproductive cycle to begin, it triggers a mechanism through which hundreds of miles of coral reef can change colour within hours.

Another more immediately observable example is the way women living together will very often synchronise in their menstrual cycles. This is not a fascistic scheme of nature, supplanting the individual rhythms of each member, but a way for each member of the social grouping to become more attuned and responsive to the subtle shifts in one another's physical and emotional states. Each member has more, not less, influence over the whole.

These models of phase-locking and self-similarity, first studied by the chaos mathematicians but eventually adopted by the culture of the internet, also seemed to be reflected in the ever-expanding mediaspace. The notion of remote high leverage points (a butterfly flapping its wings in Brazil leading to a hurricane in New York) was now proven every day by a datasphere capable of transmitting a single image globally in a matter of minutes. A black man being beaten by white cops in Los Angeles is captured on a home video camera and appears on television sets around the globe overnight. Eventually, this 30-second segment of police brutality leads to full-scale urban rioting in a dozen American cities.

These models for interactivity and coordinated behaviour may have been launched in the laboratory, but they were first embraced by countercultures. Psychedelics enthusiasts (people who either ingested substances such as LSD or found themselves inspired by the art, writing and expression of the culture associated with these drugs) found themselves drawn to technologies that were capable of reproducing both the visual effects of their hallucinations as well as the sense of newfound connection with others.

Similarly, the computer and internet galvanised certain strains of both the pagan and the grassroots 'do-it-yourself' countercultures as the 'cyberpunk' movement, which was dedicated to altering reality through technology, together. Only now are the social effects of these technologies being considered by political scientists for what they may teach us about public opinion and civic engagement.

The underlying order of apparently chaotic systems in mathematics and in nature suggests that systems can behave in a fashion mutually beneficial to all members, even without a command hierarchy. The term scientists use to describe the natural self-organisation of a community is 'emergence'.

As we have seen, until rather recently, most observers thought of a colony of beings, say ants, as receiving their commands from the top: the queen. It turns out that this is not the way individuals in the complex insect society know what to do. It is not a hierarchical system, they don't receive orders the way soldiers do in an army. The amazing organisation of an anthill 'emerges' from the bottom up, in a collective demonstration of each ant's evolved instincts. In a sense, it is not organised at all since there is no central bureaucracy. The collective behaviour of the colony is an emergent phenomenon.

Likewise, the slime mould growing in damp fields and forests all around us can exhibit remarkably coordinated behaviour. Most of the time, the sludge-like collection of micro-organisms go about their business quite independently of one another, each one foraging for food and moving about on its own. But when conditions worsen, food becomes scarce or the forest floor becomes dry, the formerly distinct creatures coalesce into a single being. The large mass of slime moves about, amassing the moisture of the collective, until it finds a more hospitable region of forest, and then breaks up again into individual creatures. The collective behaviour is an emergent trait, learned through millennia of evolution. But it is only activated when the group is under threat. The processes allowing for these alternative strategies are still being scrutinised by scientists, who are only beginning to come to grips with the implications of these findings in understanding other emergent systems from cities to civilisations.

At first glance, the proposition that human civilisation imitates the behaviour of slime mould is preposterous, an evolutionary leap backwards. An individual human consciousness is infinitely more advanced than that of a single slime mould micro-organism. But a coordinated human meta-organism is not to be confused with the highly structured visions of a 'super organism' imagined in the philosophical precursors to fascism in the nineteenth and twentieth centuries. Rather, thanks to the feedback and iteration offered by our new interactive networks, we aspire towards a highly articulated and dynamic body politic: a genuinely networked democracy, capable of accepting and maintaining a multiplicity of points of view, instead of seeking premature resolution and the oversimplification that comes with it.

This is why it appeared that the decision to grant the public open access to the internet in the early 1990s would herald a new era of teledemocracy, political activism and a reinstatement of the collective will into public affairs. The emergence of a networked culture, accompanied by an ethic of media literacy, open discussion and direct action, held the promise of a more responsive political system wherever it spread.

But most efforts at such teledemocracy so far, such as former Clinton pollster Dick Morris's website www.vote.com, or even the somewhat effective political action site www.moveon.org, are simply new versions of the public opinion poll. Billing themselves as the next phase in a truly populist and articulated body politic, the sites amount to little more than an opportunity for politicians to glean the gist of a few more uninformed, knee-jerk reactions to the issue of the day. Vote.com, as the name suggests, reduces representative democracy to just another marketing survey. Even if it is just the framework for a much more substantial future version, it is based on a fundamentally flawed vision of push-button politics. That's the vision shared by most teledemocracy champions today.

So what went wrong? Why didn't networked politics lead to a genuinely networked engagement in public affairs?

Interference in the emergence

First, by casting itself in the role of cultural and institutional watchdog, governments, particularly in the United States, became internet society's enemy. Though built with mostly US government dollars, the internet's growth into a public medium seemed to be impeded by the government's own systemic aversion to the kinds of information, images and ideas that the network spread. The government's fear of hackers was compounded by a fear of pornography and the fear of terrorism. The result was a tirade of ill-conceived legislation that made internet enthusiasts' blood boil. New decency laws aimed at curbing pornography (which were ultimately struck down) elicited cries of curtailment on free speech. Unsubstantiated and bungled raids on young hackers and their families turned law enforcement into the Keystone Cops of cyberspace and the US Justice Department into a sworn enemy of the shareware community's most valuable members. Misguided (and unsuccessful) efforts at preventing the dissemination of cryptography protocols across national boundaries turned corporate developers into government-haters as well. (This tradition of government interference in the rise of a community-driven internet is contrasted by the early participation of the UK's Labour government in the funding of internet opportunities there, such as community centres and public timeshare terminals, which were initially exploited mainly by arts collectives, union organisers, and activists. Of course all this didn't play very well with the nascent UK internet industry, which saw its slow start compared with the US and other developed nations as a direct result of government over-management and anti-competitive funding policies.)

So, the US government became known as the antagonist of cyberculture. Every effort was made to diminish state control over the global telecommunications infrastructure. The internet itself, a government project, soon fell into private hands (Internic, and eventually industry consortiums). For just as a bacterium tends to grow unabated without the presence of fungus, so too does corporate power grow without the restrictive influence of government.

This in itself may not have been so terrible. E-commerce certainly has its strengths and the economic development associated with a profit-driven internet creates new reasons for new countries to get their populations online. But an interactive marketplace is not fertile soil for networked democracy or public participation. As we have seen, the objective of marketers online is to reduce interactivity, shorten consideration and induce impulsive purchases.

That's why the software and interfaces developed for the commercial webspace tended to take users' hands off the keyboard and onto the mouse. The most successful programs, for them, lead people to the 'buy' button and let them use the keyboard only to enter their credit card numbers and nothing else. The internet that grew from these development priorities, dominated by the World Wide Web instead of discussion groups, treats individuals more as consumers than as citizens. True, consumers can vote with their dollars, and that in a way feels something like direct communication with the entity in charge – the corporation. But this is not a good model for government.

Sadly, though, it's the model being used to implement these first efforts at teledemocracy. And it's why these efforts suffer from the worst symptoms of consumer culture: they focus on short-term ideals, they encourage impulsive, image-driven decision-making and they aim to convince people that their mouse-clicking is some kind of direct action. Anyone arguing against such schemes must be an enemy of the public will, an elitist. Teledemocracy is a populist revival, after all, isn't it?

Perhaps. But the system of representation on which most democracies were built was intended to buffer the effects of such populist revivals. Although they may not always (or even frequently) live up to it, our representatives' role is to think beyond short-term interests of the majority. They are elected to protect the rights of minority interests, the sorts of people and groups who are now increasingly cast as 'special interest groups'.

Achieving the promise of network democracy

The true promise of a network-enhanced democracy lies not in some form of web-driven political marketing survey, but in restoring and encouraging broader participation in some of the internet's more interactive forums. Activists of all stripes now have the freedom and facility to network and organise across vast geographical, national, racial and even ideological differences. And they've begun to do so. The best evidence we have that something truly new is going on is our mainstream media's inability to understand it. Major American news outlets are still incapable of acknowledging the tremendous breadth of the World Trade Organisation (WTO) protest movement because of the multiplicity of cooperating factions within it. Unable to draw out a single, simplified rationale that encompasses the logic of each and every protestor, traditional media storytellers conclude that there is no logic at all. (Just as I am writing this section, a newscaster on CNBC, reporting from a WTO demonstration, is condescendingly laughing at the word 'neo-liberal' on a placard, believing that the teen protestor holding it has invented the term!) In actuality, the multi-faceted rationale underlying the WTO protests confirms both their broad-based support as well as the quite evolved capacity of its members to coalesce across previously unimaginable ideological chasms. Indeed, these obsolete ideologies are themselves falling away as a new dynamic emerges from nascent political organism.

For politicians who mean to lead more effectively in such an environment, the interactive solution may well be a new emphasis on education, where elected leaders use the internet to engage with constituents and justify the decisions they have made on our behalf, rather than simply soliciting our moment-to-moment opinions. Politicians cannot hope to reduce the collective will of their entire constituencies into a series of yes or no votes on the issues put before them. They can, however, engage the public in an ongoing exploration and dialogue on issues and their impacts, and attempt to provide a rationale for their roles in the chamber in which they participate. They must accept that their constituents are capable of comprehending legislative bodies as functioning organisms. In doing so, politicians will relieve themselves of the responsibility for hyping or spinning their decisions and instead use their time with the public to engage them in the evolution of the legislative process. Like teachers and religious leaders, whose roles as authority figures have been diminished by their students' and congregants' direct access to formerly secret data, politicians too must learn to function more like partners than parents.

In doing so, they will leave the certainty of twentieth-century political ideologies behind, and admit to the open-ended and uncertain process of societal co-authorship. Whatever model they choose must shun static ideologies, and instead acknowledge the evolutionary process through which anything resembling progress is made.

6. Open source: Imagining network democracy

One model for the open-ended and participatory process through which legislation might occur in a networked democracy can be found in the 'open source' software movement. Faced with the restrictive practices of the highly competitive software developers, and the pitifully complex and inefficient operating systems such as Microsoft Windows that this process produces, a global community of programmers decided to find a better development philosophy for themselves. They founded one based in the original values of the shareware software development community, concluding that proprietary software is crippled by the many efforts to keep its underlying code a secret and locked down. Many users don't even know that a series of arbitrary decisions have been made about the software they use. They don't know it can be changed. They simply adjust.

By publishing software along with its source code, open source developers encourage one another to correct each other's mistakes, and improve upon each other's work. Rather than competing they collaborate, and don't hide the way their programs work. As a result, everyone is invited to change the underlying code and the software can evolve with the benefit of a multiplicity of points of view. Of course this depends on a lot of preconditions. Participants in an open source collaboration must be educated in the field they are developing. People cannot expect to be able to understand and edit the code underlying any system until they have taken the time and spent the necessary energy to penetrate it. Very often, as in the case of computer software, this also depends on open standards so that the code is accessible to all. But it is also true of many other systems. If those who hope to engage in the revision of our societal models are not educated by those who developed what is already in place, they will spend most of their time inefficiently reverse-engineering existing structures in an effort to understand them. Progress can only be made if new minds are educated in the current languages, exposed to the rationale for all decisions that have been made and invited to test new methods and structures.

Those who are invited to re-evaluate our social and political structures in such a way will stand the best chance of gaining the perspective necessary to see the emergent properties of such systems, as well as avenues for active participation in them. If no one is invited then the first harbingers of emergent paradigms will be those who have been motivated to train themselves in spite of the obstacles set in front of them by those who hope to maintain exclusive control over the code. The new models they come up with may, as a result, end up looking much more like old-style revolutions than true renaissances.

The implementation of an open source democracy will require us to dig deep into the very code of our legislative processes, and then rebirth it in the new context of our networked reality. It will require us to assume, at least temporarily, that nothing at all is too sacred to be questioned, reinterpreted and modified. But in doing so, we will be enabled to bring democracy through its current crisis and into its next stage of development.

But, like literacy, the open source ethos and process are hard if not impossible to control once they are unleashed. Once people are invited to participate in, say, the coding of a software program, they begin to question just how much of the rest of our world is open for discussion. They used to see software as an established and inviolable thing – something married to the computer. A given circumstance. With an open source awareness, they are free to discover that the codes of the software have been arranged by people, sometimes with agendas that hadn't formerly been apparent. One of the most widespread realisations accompanying the current renaissance is that a lot of what has been taken for granted as 'hardware' is, in fact, 'software' capable of being reprogrammed. They tend to begin to view everything that was formerly set in stone – from medical practices to the Bible – as social constructions and subject to revision. Likewise as public awareness of emergence theory increases, people are beginning to observe their world differently, seeing its principles in evidence everywhere. Formerly esoteric subjects such as urban design or monetary policy become much more central as the public comes to recognise the power of these planning specialties to establish the rules through which society actually comes into existence.

This marks a profound shift in our relationship to law and governance. We move from simply following the law to understanding the law, to actually feeling capable of writing the law: adhering to the map to understanding the map, to drawing our own. At the very least, we are aware that the choices made on our behalf have the ability to shape our future reality and that these choices are not ordained but implemented by people just like us.

Unlike in the 1960s, when people questioned their authorities in the hope of replacing them (revolution), today's activists are forcing us to re-evaluate the premise underlying top-down authority as an organising principle (renaissance). Bottom-up organisational models, from slime mould to WTO protests, seem better able to address today's participatory sensibility. Indeed, the age of irony may be over, not just because the American dream has been interrupted by terrorism and economic shocks but because media-savvy Westerners are no longer satisfied with understanding current events through the second-hand cynical musings of magazine journalists. They want to engage more directly and they see almost every set of rules as up for reinterpretation and re-engineering.

Applying the theory

So what happens when the open source development model is applied to, say, the economy? In the United States, it would mean coming to appreciate the rules of the economic game for what they are: rules. Operating in a closed source fashion, the right to actually produce currency is held exclusively by the Federal Reserve. Quietly removed from any relationship to real money such as gold or silver by Richard Nixon in the early 1970s, US currency now finds its value in pure social construction. Whether or not we know it, we all participate in the creation of its value by competing for dollars against one another. For example, when a person or business borrows money from the bank (an agent, in a sense, of the Federal Reserve) in the form of a mortgage they must eventually pay the bank back two or three times the original borrowed amount. These additional funds are not printed into existence, but must be won from others in the closed source system. Likewise, every time a student wants to buy one of my books, he must go out into the economy and earn or win some of these arbitrarily concocted tokens, US currency, in order to do it. Our transaction is brokered by the Federal Reserve, which has a monopoly on this closed source currency.

Meanwhile, the actual value of this currency, and the effort required to obtain it, is decided much more by market speculators than its actual users. Speculation accounts for over 90 per cent of US currency transactions in any given day. By this measure, real spending and the real economy are a tiny and secondary function of money: the dog is being wagged by its tail.

What if currency were to become open source? In some communities it already is. They are not printing counterfeit bills but catalysing regional economies through the use of local currencies, locally created 'scrip' that can be exchanged throughout a particular region in lieu of Federal Reserve notes or real cash. The use of these currencies, as promoted by organisations such as the E.F. Schumacher Society, has been shown to accelerate the exchange of goods and services in a region by increasing the purchasing power of its members. There is no Federal Reserve surcharge on the creation and maintenance of cash, and no danger of government currency depreciation due to matters that have nothing to do with actual production and consumption.

Like any other bottom-up system, the creation of local currency develops transactional models appropriate to the scale of the actual transactions and the communities in which they occur. While Federal notes, or euros for that matter, might be appropriate for a merchant to use across state or national boundaries, local currencies make for greater fluidity and accountability between members of the same community.

Thanks to the dynamic relationships permitted in a networked society, we need not choose between local and closed currencies. A post-renaissance perspective on economic issues has room for both to exist, simultaneously functioning on different orders of magnitude.

In a society modelled on open source ideals, 'think globally, act locally' becomes more than just a catchphrase. The relationship of an individual or local community's action to the whole system can be experienced quite readily. For example, an open source software developer who writes just a few useful lines of code, say the protocol for enabling infrared communications to work on the Linux operating system, will see his or her contribution interpolated into the kernel of the operating system and then spread to everyone who uses it. He has done more than distributed a line of computer code. He has also enabled thousands of people using Linux to connect cell phones, PDAs and other devices to their computers for the first time. And he did it from his home, in his spare time.

Likewise, a developer who leaves a security hole open in a piece of software quite dramatically sees the results of his action when a software 'worm', written by a computer criminal, penetrates the mail files of thousands of users, sending replicates of itself throughout the internet, sometimes for years to come.

Members of an open source community are able to experience how their actions affect the whole. As a result, they become more conscious of how their moment-to-moment decisions can be better aligned with the larger issues with which they are concerned. A programmer concerned with energy consumption and the environment might take time to consider how a particular screen-saver routine impacts the total energy consumption pattern of a particular monitor. The programmer already understands that if the code is used on millions of machines, each effort to reduce energy consumption by a minuscule amount can amplify into tremendous energy savings. (Indeed, it has been calculated that the energy required to power all the televisions and computers in America that are currently in sleep mode equals the output of an entire average-size power plant.)

The experience of open source development, or even just the acceptance of its value as a model for others, provides real-life practice for the deeper change in perspective required of us if we are to move into a more networked and emergent understanding of our world. The local community must be experienced as a place to implement policies, incrementally, that will eventually have an effect on the whole. For example, the environmental advocate who worries about the Brazilian rainforest will quit smoking himself before racing off to the next rally held to save the lungs of the planet. The woman organising against genetic engineering in agriculture will refuse to let her children eat at McDonald's, even if it requires them to bring their own lunch to a friend's birthday party. A consistency between belief and behaviour becomes the only way to make our designs on reality real.

Closed source: no justice, no power

An open source model for participatory, bottom-up and emergent policy will force us, or allow us, to confront the issues of our time more directly. Using the logic of a computer programmer, when we find we can't solve a problem by attacking one level of societal software, we proceed to the next level down. If necessary we dig all the way down to the machine language.

For instance, today's misunderstood energy crisis provides a glaring example of the liability of closed source policy-making. The

Western world is unnecessarily addicted to fossil fuels and other energy commodities not because alternative energy sources are unavailable, but because alternative business models for energy production cannot be fully considered without disrupting the world's most powerful corporations and economies. It really is as simple as that.

Solar, geothermal and other renewable energy sources are quite ready for deployment in a wide variety of applications. They are not encouraged, not through tax policies nor through venture capital, because they don't make sense to an industry and economy that has based its business model on the exploitation of fixed and precious resources: a closed source model. As a result, we are suffering through a potentially irreversible environmental crisis, as well as a geopolitical conflict that is already spinning wildly out of control.

The maintenance of such imbalances is dependent on closed source processes. The power of puppet dictators in the oil-producing Middle East is perpetuated not just by US warplanes, but by their own economies which derive all their wealth through the exploitation of resources. Were these nations required to compete in the global marketplace through the production of goods or services, then a passive, uneducated population would no longer bring their monarchs the wealth to which they are accustomed. As it is, the peasants need only be educated enough to dig. And the closed source mentality travels all the way around the distribution cycle. Nowhere is the closed source imperative of an oil-based economy more evident than in the appointment, by America's judicial branch (though not its population), of a President to represent the oil industry.

7. Conclusion

The new transparency offered by the interactive mediaspace allows even the casually interested reader to learn how the West's foreign and domestic policies have been twisted to a perverse caricature of themselves. I do not wish here to beat the drum for a partisan revolution. Instead, I am to demonstrate how a growing willingness to engage with the underlying code of the democratic process could eventually manifest in a widespread call for revisions to our legal, economic and political structures on an unprecedented scale, except in the cases of full-fledged revolution. Transparency in media makes information available to those who never had access to it before. Access to media technology empowers those same people to discuss how they might want to change the status quo. Finally, networking technologies allow for online collaboration in the implementation of new models, and the very real-world organisation of social activism and relief efforts. The good news, for those within the power structure today, is that we are not about to enter a phase of revolution, but one of renaissance. We are heading not towards a toppling of the democratic, parliamentary or legislative processes, but towards their reinvention in a new, participatory context. In a sense, the people are becoming a new breed of wonk, capable of engaging with government and power structures in an entirely new fashion. The current regime, in the broadest sense, will have ended up being the true and lasting one if it can get its head and policies around these renaissance modalities of increased dimensionality, emergence, scalability and participation.

My advice? Don't beat them. Let them join you. Choose to believe that the renaissance I am describing has already taken place. Instead of looking forward to a day when justice will be won, declare that we are living in a just world right now. Declare that we are simply fighting for more justice.

Movements, as such, are obsolete. They are incompatible with a renaissance sensibility because of the narrative style of their intended unfolding. They yearn forward towards salvation in the manner of utopians or fundamentalists: an increasing number of people are becoming aware of how movements of all stripes justify tremendous injustice in the name of that deferred future moment. People are actually taken out of their immediate experience and their connection to the political process as they put their heads down and do battle. It becomes not worth believing in anything.

This is why we have to advocate living in the now in order to effect any real change. There should be no postponement of joy. Once we start down this path, there can be no stopping. We begin to see the unreality of money. We begin to see how 'salvation' has been traded in for 'retirement' as the new ultimate goal for which Westerners suspend their lives and their ethics. (People work for companies they hate, and then invest in corporations whose ethics they detest, in order to guarantee a good retirement.) We see the artificial obstacles to appropriate energy policy, international relations, urban planning and affordable healthcare as what they are: artificial. Meanwhile, what we can accomplish presents itself on a much more realistic scale when we engage with it in the moment and on a local level.

Yes, political structures do need to be changed. But we may have to let their replacements emerge from the myriad of new relationships that begin to spawn once people are acting and communicating in the present, and on a realistic scale, instead of talking about a fictional future.

The underlying premise is still dependent on the notion of progress. Indeed, things must get better or there's no point to any of it. But our understanding of progress must be disengaged from the false goal of growth, or the even more dangerous ideal of salvation. Our understanding must be reconnected with the very basic measure of social justice: how many people are able to participate?

Our marketing experts tell us that they are failing in their efforts to advertise to internet users and cultural progressives because this new and resistant psychographic simply wants to engage, authentically, in social experiences. This should sound like good news to anyone who authentically wants to extend our collective autonomy. This population is made up not of customers to whom you must sell, or even constituents to whom you must pander, but of partners on whom you can rely and with whom you can act.

Treat them as such, and you might be surprised by how much you get done together.

Notes

1   Karen Armstrong, *A History of God* (London: Vintage, 1999).

2   *First Monday*, 'The High-Tech Gift Economy'. Richard Sambrook, 1998, (http://www.firstmonday.dk/ issues/issue3_12/barbrook/).

3   Douglas Rushkoff, *Cyberia: Life in the Trenches of Hyperspace* (Flamingo, 1994).

4   *Wired Magazine*, July 1997 (see http://www.wired.com/wired/ archive/5.07/longboom_pr.html).

Open Access Publishing Licence

DEM☾S

THE WORK (AS DEFINED BELOW) IS PROVIDED UNDER THE TERMS OF THIS LICENCE ("LICENCE"). THE WORK IS PROTECTED BY COPYRIGHT AND/OR OTHER APPLICABLE LAW. ANY USE OF THE WORK OTHER THAN AS AUTHORIZED UNDER THIS LICENCE IS PROHIBITED. BY EXERCISING ANY RIGHTS TO THE WORK PROVIDED HERE, YOU ACCEPT AND AGREE TO BE BOUND BY THE TERMS OF THIS LICENCE. DEMOS GRANTS YOU THE RIGHTS CONTAINED HERE IN CONSIDERATION OF YOUR ACCEPTANCE OF SUCH TERMS AND CONDITIONS.

1. Definitions

a. "Collective Work" means a work, such as a periodical issue, anthology or encyclopedia, in which the Work in its entirety in unmodified form, along with a number of other contributions, constituting separate and independent works in themselves, are assembled into a collective whole. A work that constitutes a Collective Work will not be considered a Derivative Work (as defined below) for the purposes of this Licence.

b. "Derivative Work" means a work based upon the Work or upon the Work and other pre-existing works, such as a musical arrangement, dramatization, fictionalization, motion picture version, sound recording, art reproduction, abridgment, condensation, or any other form in which the Work may be recast, transformed, or adapted, except that a work that constitutes a Collective Work or a translation from English into another language will not be considered a Derivative Work for the purpose of this Licence.

c. "Licensor" means the individual or entity that offers the Work under the terms of this Licence.
d. "Original Author" means the individual or entity who created the Work.
e. "Work" means the copyrightable work of authorship offered under the terms of this Licence.
f. "You" means an individual or entity exercising rights under this Licence who has not previously violated the terms of this Licence with respect to the Work, or who has received express permission from DEMOS to exercise rights under this Licence despite a previous violation.

2. Fair Use Rights. Nothing in this licence is intended to reduce, limit, or restrict any rights arising from fair use, first sale or other limitations on the exclusive rights of the copyright owner under copyright law or other applicable laws.

3. Licence Grant. Subject to the terms and conditions of this Licence, Licensor hereby grants You a worldwide, royalty-free, non-exclusive, perpetual (for the duration of the applicable copyright) licence to exercise the rights in the Work as stated below:

a. to reproduce the Work, to incorporate the Work into one or more Collective Works, and to reproduce the Work as incorporated in the Collective Works;

b. to distribute copies or phonorecords of, display publicly, perform publicly, and perform publicly by means of a digital audio transmission the Work including as incorporated in Collective Works;

The above rights may be exercised in all media and formats whether now known or hereafter devised. The above rights include the right to make such modifications as are technically necessary to exercise the rights in other media and formats. All rights not expressly granted by Licensor are hereby reserved.

4. Restrictions. The licence granted in Section 3 above is expressly made subject to and limited by the following restrictions:

a. You may distribute, publicly display, publicly perform, or publicly digitally perform the Work only under the terms of this Licence, and You must include a copy of, or the Uniform Resource Identifier for, this Licence with every copy or phonorecord of the Work You distribute, publicly display, publicly perform, or publicly digitally perform. You may not offer or impose any terms on the Work that alter or restrict the terms of this Licence or the recipients' exercise of the rights granted hereunder. You may not sublicence the Work. You must keep intact all notices that refer to this Licence and to the disclaimer of warranties. You may not distribute, publicly display, publicly perform, or publicly digitally perform the Work with any technological measures that control access or use of the Work in a manner inconsistent with the terms of this Licence Agreement. The above applies to the Work as incorporated in a Collective Work, but this does not require the Collective Work apart from the Work itself to be made subject to the terms of this Licence. If You create a Collective Work, upon notice from any Licencor You must, to the extent practicable, remove from the Collective Work any reference to such Licensor or the Original Author, as requested.

b. You may not exercise any of the rights granted to You in Section 3 above in any manner that is primarily intended for or directed toward commercial advantage or private monetary compensation. The exchange of the Work for other copyrighted works by means of digital file-sharing or otherwise shall not be considered to be intended for or directed toward commercial advantage or private monetary compensation, provided there is no payment of any monetary compensation in connection with the exchange of copyrighted works.

c. If you distribute, publicly display, publicly perform, or publicly digitally perform the Work or any Collective Works, You must keep intact all copyright notices for the Work and give the Original Author credit reasonable to the medium or means You are utilizing by conveying the name (or pseudonym if applicable) of the Original Author if supplied; the title of the Work if supplied. Such credit may be implemented in any reasonable manner; provided, however, that in the case of a Collective Work, at a minimum such credit will appear where any other comparable authorship credit appears and in a manner at least as prominent as such other comparable authorship credit.

5. Representations, Warranties and Disclaimer

a. By offering the Work for public release under this Licence, Licensor represents and warrants that, to the best of Licensor's knowledge after reasonable inquiry:

i. Licensor has secured all rights in the Work necessary to grant the licence rights hereunder and to permit the lawful exercise of the rights granted hereunder without You having any obligation to pay any royalties, compulsory licence fees, residuals or any other payments;

ii. The Work does not infringe the copyright, trademark, publicity rights, common law rights or any other right of any third party or constitute defamation, invasion of privacy or other tortious injury to any third party.

b. EXCEPT AS EXPRESSLY STATED IN THIS LICENCE OR OTHERWISE AGREED IN WRITING OR REQUIRED BY APPLICABLE LAW, THE WORK IS LICENCED ON AN "AS IS" BASIS, WITHOUT WARRANTIES OF ANY KIND, EITHER EXPRESS OR IMPLIED INCLUDING, WITHOUT LIMITATION, ANY WARRANTIES REGARDING THE CONTENTS OR ACCURACY OF THE WORK.

6. Limitation on Liability. EXCEPT TO THE EXTENT REQUIRED BY APPLICABLE LAW, AND EXCEPT FOR DAMAGES ARISING FROM LIABILITY TO A THIRD PARTY RESULTING FROM BREACH OF THE WARRANTIES IN SECTION 5, IN NO EVENT WILL LICENSOR BE LIABLE TO YOU ON ANY LEGAL THEORY FOR ANY SPECIAL, INCIDENTAL, CONSEQUENTIAL, PUNITIVE OR EXEMPLARY DAMAGES ARISING OUT OF THIS LICENCE OR THE USE OF THE WORK, EVEN IF LICENSOR HAS BEEN ADVISED OF THE POSSIBILITY OF SUCH DAMAGES.

7. Termination

a. This Licence and the rights granted hereunder will terminate automatically upon any breach by You of the terms of this Licence. Individuals or entities who have received Collective Works from You under this Licence, however, will not have their licences terminated provided such individuals or entities remain in full compliance with those licences. Sections 1, 2, 5, 6, 7, and 8 will survive any termination of this Licence.

b. Subject to the above terms and conditions, the licence granted here is perpetual (for the duration of the applicable copyright in the Work). Notwithstanding the above, Licensor reserves the right to release the Work under different licence terms or to stop distributing the Work at any time; provided, however that any such election will not serve to withdraw this Licence (or any other licence that has been, or is required to be, granted under the terms of this Licence), and this Licence will continue in full force and effect unless terminated as stated above.

8. Miscellaneous

a. Each time You distribute or publicly digitally perform the Work or a Collective Work, DEMOS offers to the recipient a licence to the Work on the same terms and conditions as the licence granted to You under this Licence.

b. If any provision of this Licence is invalid or unenforceable under applicable law, it shall not affect the validity or enforceability of the remainder of the terms of this Licence, and without further action by the parties to this agreement, such provision shall be reformed to the minimum extent necessary to make such provision valid and enforceable.

c. No term or provision of this Licence shall be deemed waived and no breach consented to unless such waiver or consent shall be in writing and signed by the party to be charged with such waiver or consent.

d. This Licence constitutes the entire agreement between the parties with respect to the Work licensed here. There are no understandings, agreements or representations with respect to the Work not specified here. Licensor shall not be bound by any additional provisions that may appear in any communication from You. This Licence may not be modified without the mutual written agreement of DEMOS and You.